Stage 2 Paper 7

*Management Science
Applications*

First edition 1996
Fifth edition January 2000

ISBN 0 7517 3492 6 (previous edition 07517 3476 4)

British Library Cataloguing-in-Publication Data

A catalogue record for this book
is available from the British Library

Published by

BPP Publishing Limited
Aldine House, Aldine Place
London W12 8AW

www.bpp.com

Printed in Great Britain by
Ashford Colour Press, Gosport, Hampshire

If you use CIMA **Passcards**, you can be sure that the time you spend on final revision for your **Year 2000 exams** is time well spent.

- They **save you time**: following the structure of the BPP Study Text for Paper 7, important facts on key exam topics are summarised for you

- They incorporate diagrams to kick start your memory

- They are pocket-sized: you can run through them **anytime** and **anywhere**

CIMA **Passcards** focus on the exam you will be facing.

- They highlight which topics have been examined - and when

- They provide you with suggestions on subject examinability, given past exams and the direction the examiner appears to be taking, in **exam focus points**

- They give you useful **exam hints** that can earn you those vital extra marks in the exam

Run through the complete set of **Passcards** as often as you can during your final revision period. The day before the exam, try to go through the **Passcards** again. You will then be well on your way to passing your exams. **Good luck**

Contents

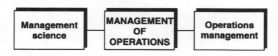

Management science

This is the use of quantitative techniques *to help solve the problems of running a business*. Quantitative techniques that have been examined in the specimen paper and the ten exams that have been set so far are as follows.

Network analysis	(4)	Decision trees	(5)
Pareto analysis	(4)	Linear programming	(7)
Sampling	(8)	Simulation	(3)
Management report	(5)	Time series and	
Control charts	(2)	exponential	
Chi-squared tests	(7)	smoothing	(2)
Stock control	(7)	Linear regression	(6)
NPV and IRR	(6)	Learning curves	(1)
Mortgages	(3)	Market demand	
Reserve funds	(2)	analysis and pricing	
Capital replacement	(3)	policies	(9)

(Bracketed numbers show how many times the topic has come up.)

Some questions ask for a report with supporting figures and diagrams, so the choice of technique is left up to you.

Most questions award at least a quarter or more of the total marks available for written commentary on the figures you are asked to calculate.

- You are very unlikely to pass the exam if you do not attempt to answer these parts of the question

- Your task is to convince the examiner that you can *help solve business problems*, not just that you can use a calculator

> *Exam focus.* Typical requirements of this kind are 'Explain the
> meaning of your answer in non-technical terms'; 'Write a brief
> management report of your findings', 'Describe the implications of
> your results'. Most of the many marks available can be earned
> simply by making some common-sense remarks such as 'The
> figures show that marketing should target different types of
> adventure holiday at different age groups'.

The emphasis of the exam reflects the fact that management
science techniques are not used widely enough in business,
largely because those who are supposed to be able to use
them (people like you) fail to develop the communication skills
necessary to persuade other managers of their value.

> *Exam focus.* One question in the May 1996 exam asked you to
> describe and explain the use of two from four management
> science techniques.

Operations management   11/95

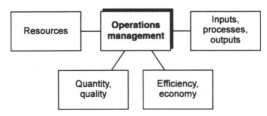

This is the management of resources so as to produce, on
time, the *required quantity* of products or services, of the
correct quality or standard, by the most *efficient and
economical* means.

- *Resources* are the four 'M's, people, materials, machines
  and money, plus space, time and information

- Producing goods and services is a matter of taking *inputs* and *processing* them so that they become *outputs*

Any product or service can be analysed in these terms: try it with anything you can see right now.

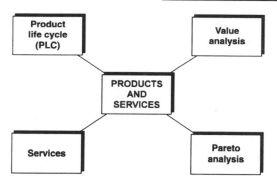

Product life cycle (PLC)   5/99

The PLC concept assumes that a product or service goes through several stages in its history.

- Introduction

- Growth

- Maturity

- Decline

Not everyone accepts that the PLC concept is valid but it does provide a convenient framework for analysing the 'operations' aspects of different businesses.

- For example, when a new product is launched (introduction) we might expect the following

  - *Quality* to be on the poor side
  - *Production costs* and *prices* to be high
  - *Advertising and sales promotion* costs to be high
  - Few or no *competitors*

- But for a company that produces 'mature' products, we might expect the following

  o *Quality* will be at its best

  o *Production costs* will be low because capacity utilisation will be at an optimum

  o *Prices* will be relatively low but sales volume high

  o Repeat-buying and customer loyalty will be the crucial concerns of *marketing*

  o *Competition* will be fierce

The key point is that as products and services develop, so the nature of the operations and management decisions surrounding them will also develop.

Exam focus. You may be tested specifically on the PLC but even if not, you should be able to see its relevance to *any* business scenario. For example, in a scenario involving the introduction of a new product, all of the written 'interpretation' parts of your answers will benefit if you keep in mind the sort of issues that might be expected to arise in this situation: teething troubles with the product, less than full utilisation of capacity, the difficulty of setting a price when there is no competition and so on. This is the sort of thing we mean by general business sense.

Value analysis

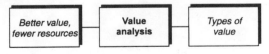

Better value, fewer resources

Value analysis looks at the factors that affect the costs of a product or service and tries to find ways of making the same or better 'value' of product or service more economically.

(Note that this is very similar to the explanation that we gave earlier of operations management as a whole.)

Types of value

Four types of value are recognised.

- *Cost value*: the cost of producing and selling an item

- *Exchange value*: the market value

- *Use value*: the purpose the item fulfils (often difficult to quantify)

- *Esteem value*: the prestige the customer attaches to the item (again, often difficult to quantify)

A business will wish to reduce cost value and increase the other types of value. This may be done by changing product design or materials and/or changing production or delivery methods.

> *Exam focus*. The quality of an organisation's output is one of the key concerns of modern business. See Chapter 8.

Pareto analysis   *11/95, 5/96, 11/97*

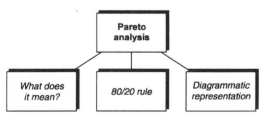

In questions set so far, by Pareto analysis the MSA examiner means finding out what proportion of a total is represented by each of the individual things making up the total. For example, here is a Pareto analysis of sales.

Product	Sales	Sales	Cumulative sales	Cumulative sales
	Units	%	Units	%
A	1,000	43	1,000	43
B	800	35	1,800	78
C	500	22	2,300	100
Total	2,300	100		

A similar analysis could be done for any other aspect of product data: contribution, cost, complaints or whatever.

What does it mean?

- In questions set so far, it has been necessary to do a Pareto analysis of sales levels as compared with contribution or amount of stock held

- Typically this reveals that the products/divisions that sell the most are different from the products/divisions that provide the highest contribution or hold the highest levels of stocks

- This may suggest management action such as the revision of pricing policy or the discontinuance of certain products

---

Exam focus. Pareto analysis questions usually require the calculation of cumulative percentages. In order to save time in an examination remember to use the 'constant mode' on your calculator when dividing to obtain the percentages.

80/20 rule

- Strictly speaking 'Pareto' is synonymous with the 80/20 rule - 80% of something is accounted for by 20% of something else (for example 80% of stock value is represented by only 20% of stock items)

- This should not be interpreted too literally - the basic principle is that a few items or activities are often core to an organisation's fortunes while the majority are only peripheral

Exam focus. In the May 1996 exam, for example, $33^{1}/_{3}$% of divisions contributed 70% of total turnover.

Diagrammatic representation

Pareto curve of sales

Pareto analysis

Sales / *Contribution*

Sales column (bottom to top):
- A 29%
- B 20%
- C 12%
- D 11%
- E 10%
- F 6%
- G 5%
- H 4%
- I 3%

Contribution column (bottom to top):
- B 37%
- C 19%
- D 11%
- F 9%
- A 8%
- H 6%
- G 5%
- I 4%
- E 1%

Services

Services are characterised by four aspects.

- Intangibility

- Simultaneity

- Heterogeneity

- Perishability

Car insurance or a train journey are good examples. In terms of what businesses do, there are very few pure products or pure services: organisations sell *benefits* that are services with products linked to them or products linked with services.

It is possible to distinguish between three different types of service organisation.

- Professional services: for example, accountants
- Mass services: for example, British Airways
- Service shops: for example, a bank

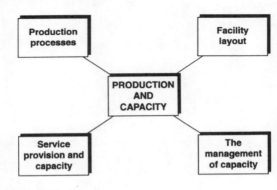

Production processes

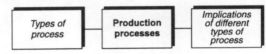

Types of process   5/98

The main types of production process are as follows.

- *Projects*: large-scale single items like the Channel Tunnel

- *Jobs*: like a project but shorter-term and on a smaller scale (eg a tailor-made suit)

- *Batch production*: a number of similar items such as a batch of size 12 dresses in the same style and material

- *Line production*: where parts of the production facility are permanently dedicated to the production of single items, for example Ford Escorts

- *Continuous processing*: this is the sort of production method used in an oil refinery where basic materials are turned into a single product or a variety of different products

Implications of different types of process

	Project/job	*Line/continuous*
Product	One-off, made to order, non-standard, diverse	High-volume, made to stock, highly standardised, not diverse
Market	Competition on speed and quality	Competition on price
Production	Complex, variable, flexible, long duration	Many simple repetitive tasks, little flexibility, short time-scale
People	Highly-skilled labour, technical knowledge	Relatively unskilled, people management
Equipment	General purpose	Highly specialised

Batch production on a small-scale is more like job production; on a large-scale it becomes more like line production.

Facility layout

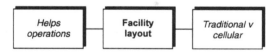

Helps operations

The way in which production facilities are laid out has an impact on the amount of *space* needed and the *time* taken to do things, and therefore on the cost of doing things.

Good layout reduces handling costs, speeds up production, helps with supervision and complies with regulations. In an office, good layout can help communication, aid co-ordination of administrative activities and improve motivation.

Traditional v cellular

Traditional layouts are either on a functional basis (assembly department, painting department) or use a product-based layout with dedicated machines.

Cellular manufacturing tries to merge the flexibility of the functional layout with the speed and productivity of the product layout. The majority of UK manufacturing companies now use cellular layouts.

The management of capacity   *5/96, 5/98*

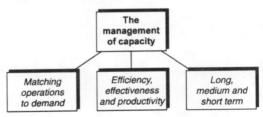

Matching operations to demand

Capacity management aims to match the level of operations to the level of demand. This involves the following.

- Estimating demand

- Ensuring that sufficient labour or machine hours are available to meet demand

Capacity is the maximum amount that can be expected to be produced in a given time, for example '10 widgets per hour'.

- Full capacity is the ideal

- Practical capacity allows for unavoidable loss of work

- Budgeted capacity is the amount of work planned

Bottlenecks occur if different parts of the process have different capacities.

Efficiency, effectiveness and productivity

- *Efficiency*
  - Getting out as much as possible for what goes in
  - Either output/input or actual output/expected output
  - You might be '105% efficient'

- *Effectiveness*
  - Getting done what was supposed to be done

- *Productivity*
  - Output/input
  - Your productivity might be '11 widgets per hour', even though capacity is regarded as '10 widgets per hour'

Long, medium and short term

In the long-term, capacity can be increased by buying more resources (more machines or more trained people).

In the medium and short term, it is necessary to do one of the following.

- Influence demand (refuse business, spread it over time)

- Stretch out existing capacity (overtime, hiring machines, deferring non-essential tasks)

An increasingly common approach if the organisation does not have sufficient internal capacity or does not want to have to buy specialist machines is to contract-out work (*outsourcing*).

> *Exam focus.* Information in this chapter could be examined in a variety of ways. A written question might ask 'what are the problems of changing from one method of production to another as the product passes through its life cycle?' A calculation question might tie in a capacity management problem with forecasting techniques and elasticity of demand. Don't pigeon-hole your knowledge.

Service provision and capacity

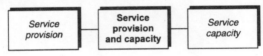

Service provision

Services are usually provided by means of 'job' type delivery (a solicitor's case) or 'batch' type delivery (a course of lectures).

Services can often only be provided at the place where the customer is at the time of provision.

- The choice of location for the 'customer interface' is therefore very important

- Harrods and Argos are two extremes: both are successful

Service capacity

Capacity is a problem because of simultaneity and perishability: running two trains rather than one at 8am on Tuesday does not produce a spare train journey for use at 7.48am on Wednesday.

- In some services, capacity can be managed by changing demand patterns

- In others (for example, a petrol station) the customer can participate and become a source of capacity

---

Exam focus. To date, production and capacity has only been examined by means of written questions. For example, candidates have been asked to describe 'management of capacity', to distinguish between 'effectiveness and efficiency' and 'long-term and short-term planning'. It is not easy to score well on these types of question, so do avoid them if at all possible.

11/99

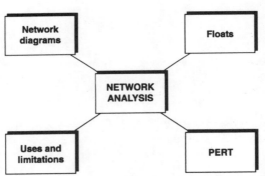

Network analysis is a technique for planning and controlling large projects such as the computerisation of a system.

> *Exam focus.* Make sure you know how to draw the diagrams and calculate floats when tackling a network analysis question in an examination, but make sure that you could also explain and comment on the technique.

The aims of network analysis from the point of view of production control are as follows.

- To identify the critical path, the activities on which must start and finish on time otherwise the project as a whole will take longer than originally anticipated

- To identify activities whose timing can be more flexible - they can either start late and/or take longer than the time specified without delaying the overall completion date, slack time on an activity being called its *float*

Network diagrams

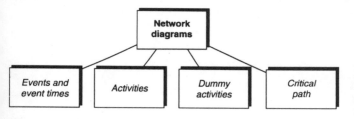

Here is a typical network diagram, followed by a key to explain the various components.

Activity	Preceded by	Duration
A	-	8
B	-	4
C	B	2
D	-	4
E	A, C, D	3
F	E	3

Always draw a rough draft of your network before presenting the final version to the examiner.

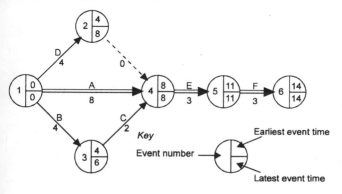

Events and event times

Events are represented by circles or 'nodes' with a number inside. An event is the end of one activity and the start of another. The top right quadrant shows the earliest event time and the bottom one shows the latest event time.

Activities

An activity is represented by an arrow. The arrow is labelled with its name (here 'B') and its duration (here 4 days or 4 weeks or whatever).

Dummy activities

- - - ►

A dummy activity is used to avoid two or more activities starting and ending on the same circle, and/or for when the start of an activity has to await the completion of two or more different activities that are on different paths. In the example, E can only start when A, C and D are finished (and A and D can both start at time 0).

Critical path

The critical path is the path that takes you from the start to the end of the network in the *longest* time. In the example, DEF = 4 + 3 + 3 = 10; AEF = 8 + 3 + 3 = 14; BCEF = 4 + 2 + 3 + 3 = 12. AEF is therefore the critical path.

Exam focus. Network diagrams should be drawn as neatly as possible in an examination - if the examiner cannot read your diagrams, he will not be able to award you any marks. Always use a sharp pencil and a ruler, and remember to label events, event times, activities (including dummy activities) and the critical path.

Floats   *11/96, 11/97, 11/98*

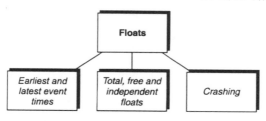

Earliest and latest event times

To calculate floats it is necessary to identify the earliest and latest time that each event can occur.

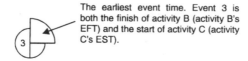

The earliest event time. Event 3 is both the finish of activity B (activity B's EFT) and the start of activity C (activity C's EST).

In a network diagram the *earliest* times are shown in the *top* right quadrant and the *latest* times in the bottom right quadrant.

- For the *earliest* times remember the following points
  - Event 1 starts at 0
  - Work from left to right
  - If more than one activity ends on the same node the earliest event time is the *highest* of all the possibilities

- For the *latest* times remember these points
  - The final event's latest time is the same as its earliest time

- o Work from right to left
- o If two or more activities start on the same node the latest event time is the *lowest* of all the possibilities

In summary - early/top/high; late/bottom/low.

Total, free and independent floats

- The *total float* for any activity is the amount of time by which its duration could be extended before it affects the total project time

- The *free float* is the amount by which an activity's duration can be increased without affecting either the total project time *or* the time available for subsequent activities

- The *independent float* of an activity is the amount by which the duration of an activity can be extended without affecting the total project time, the time available for subsequent activities *or* the time available for preceding activities

- The definitions can be summarised as follows
  - o Total float = LST – EST or LFT – EFT
  - o Free float = EST (immediate successor) – EFT
    If an activity has more than one immediate successor, the free float is the lower of all possibilities. Where dummy activities are involved, they should be treated as an extension of the main activity and the free float is calculated by referring to the EST of the next real activity
  - o Independent float = EFT – LST – D

For our example, figures are as follows.

Activity	LFT	EFT	EST	LST	Duration	Total float	Free float	Indep. float
A	8	8	0	0	8	0	0	0
B	6	4	0	2	4	2	0	0
C	8	6	4	6	2	2	2	0
D	8	*4	0	4	4	4	4	4
E	11	11	8	8	3	0	0	0
F	14	14	11	11	3	0	0	0

* The subsequent dummy activity should be treated as an extension of the activity and so EFT of D is EST plus duration = 0 + 4 = 4

Crashing

Sometimes it is possible to shorten the duration of an activity. For example, by employing an extra worker it might be possible to shorten an activity from five days to four days.

• Network analysis can be used to calculate by how much time the maximum completion time can be shortened

• Further calculations can be done to find out whether the cost of shortening a project (for example, by paying an early completion bonus) is worth the benefits

---

Exam focus. You only need to know of the existence of crashing, not how to deal with the figures.

PERT

PERT introduces uncertainty.

• Estimates are made of optimistic, most likely and pessimistic times for completion of an activity

• A formula is used to find the mean times for each activity

- Using the normal distribution it is possible to calculate the probability of a project exceeding a certain length of time

---

Exam focus. You only need to know of the existence of PERT, not how to deal with the figures.

Uses and limitations   5/95, 11/96

When a project involves carrying out a large number of different tasks, the project planner and controller has to decide the following.

- What tasks must be done before others can be started

- What tasks could be done at the same time

- What tasks must be completed on schedule if the completion date for the entire project is not to slip

Network analysis helps managers to do the following.

- Plan when to start various tasks

- Allocate resources so that the tasks can be carried out within schedule, to minimise idle resources

- Monitor actual progress

- Know when control action is needed to prevent a delay in completion of the project

Problems with network analysis are as follows.

- It may be difficult to break a project down into separate activities

- It will be difficult to estimate times for activities accurately

- The relationship between activities may not be linear eg what if something done during activity B affects the work that was done for activity A?

Exam focus. Since the MSA exam is based on a scenario it is extremely likely that a network question will ask you to explain how network analysis would help to carry out a *specific* project described in the scenario. Think about what sort of planning, scheduling and monitoring tasks would be required.

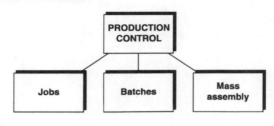

Jobs

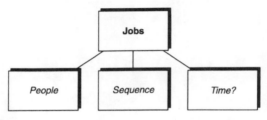

People

With jobs, work is generally allocated to *people*, depending on the skills required, other commitments and availability of facilities.

Sequence

The order (or *sequence*) in which work is done depends on circumstances. Examples include the following.

- First come, first served (at a bank counter)

- Shortest queue for facilities

- Longest job first, then next longest and so on

Time?

Estimation of *time* for activities (scheduling) is difficult for jobs because some of the tasks are unique to each job.

Batches

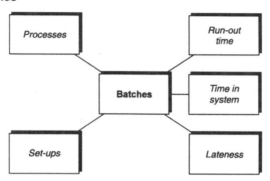

Exam focus. 'Batch and mass-assembly control' has never been examined before, but it is a new topic in the CIMA syllabus and it must be considered overdue to feature in a MSA question. On the other hand, the 'techniques' are rather vague or involve a lot of trial and error, better suited to computer analysis. A written question with a free choice of techniques may be what to expect.

Processes

With batches, work is generally allocated according to the various *processes* involved. The problem is when to send which batch through which process.

Run-out time

To minimise stock-outs work can be scheduled in order of *increasing* run-out time. For example, if current stocks are 10 units and average demand per day is 5 units, run-out time is 2 days. The shorter the run-out time, the earlier the batch should be processed.

Time in system

- If *time in the system* is an issue (eg for freshness), batches should be processed in order of increasing duration, the quickest to process being processed first so that the next batch is not left waiting any longer than necessary

- Johnson's rule can be used if batches have to be processed through two machines and time in the system is an issue
  - List processing times per batch on each machine
  - Find the shortest
  - If this time is machine 1 time, schedule the batch *first*; if it is machine 2 time, schedule it *last*
  - Repeat until all batches are scheduled

Mins	Machine	Batch	Position
15	2	A	Last
20	1	C	First
25	2	C	-
30	2	D	4th
35	2	E	3rd
40	1	B	2nd

Order of processing: C B E D A

Lateness

- If late deliveries are a problem, sequence batches in order of earliest due date first (minimise lateness).

- If lateness is inevitable it may be best to minimise the number of late deliveries

    o Arrange in order of due date and find the first late batch

    o Remove whichever of the preceding batches takes longest, revise the sequence and add the batch removed to the end

    o Repeat the second step if some batches are still late

Set-ups

- If it takes a long time to set up machines to do different things it may be possible to arrange different products into 'families' with similar set-up requirements to minimise the changes

- Cellular production is the ultimate development of this

Mass assembly

With mass assembly, processes and people are dedicated to products, so problems tend to relate to the *rate of flow* of materials to the line and shipment of final products off the line.

JIT and MRP are appropriate control techniques.

> *Exam focus.* JIT is also the method associated with *cellular production*. The examiner has said that questions will not be set on JIT and MRP.

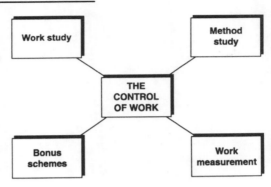

Work study

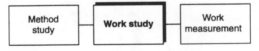

- Work study is the examination of work with a view to improving its efficiency and economy

- It has two main parts
  - Method study: how work should be done
  - Work measurement: how long it should take

- Work study is used to do the following
  - Establish standards
  - Help with job evaluation
  - Design work facilities
  - Evaluate alternative working methods
  - Develop procedures for planning and control

- It can be applied to both production and administration

- Office work study is called O&M (Organisation and Methods)

> *Exam focus.* The 'theory' of work study has not yet featured in an exam, but the numerical results of work study have formed the basis of a question.

Method study

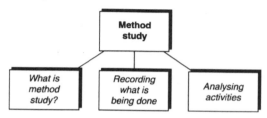

What is method study?

- A method study may be prompted by problems such as bottlenecks, idle workers, or escalating costs

- Method study aims to eliminate waste of time, effort, skills, equipment, materials, space and money .

> *Exam focus.* Method study may be linked to the product life cycle: see Chapter 2. As a business's products develop, the methods of working will need to change. For example, if a product starts to decline, working systems connected with it need to be pared down to the minimum necessary.

Recording what is being done

An investigation begins by recording data about *what* is currently being done. Recording methods include the following.

- *Procedure narrative* describes the steps involved in a procedure

- *Charts* show at a glance what is going on in a system and what faults are occurring

- *Flow process charts* record the sequence of events and movements, by person, machine or materials

> *Exam focus.* The examiner has made it clear that you will not be expected to draw charts in the exam.

Analysing activities

Once data is collected, the activities in a process can be subjected to an analysis which follows a fixed pattern. They are tested by asking five sets of questions on the following.

- Purpose
- Place
- Sequence
- Person
- Means

Work measurement

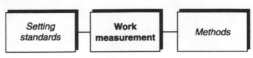

Setting standards

- Work measurement is used to set standards for the quantity and quality of work and the time spent on it

- Some kinds of work are hard to measure in terms of output, for example supervision, planning, quality control

- To express the amount of work that can be produced by a given number of personnel or equipment, some common scale of measurement is needed

- Standard time provides this, but only in situations where work is of a repetitive and fairly predictable nature

  o *Standard time* is the total time in which a job should be completed at standard performance

  o *Standard performance* is the rate of output which qualified workers will naturally achieve without over-exertion as an average over the working day or shift, provided they adhere to the specified method and provided that they are motivated to apply themselves to their work (British Standards definition)

  o What this means is that there is an optimum rate of work and one would expect the standard time for a job to be the total time taken by a qualified worker under sensible, normal conditions

Methods

Methods of work measurement most commonly used are as follows.

- *Personal observation* by a trained observer who monitors and times the task (useful for fairly simple, repetitive work)

- *Activity sampling*, which consists of taking a number of observations during the work cycle at random intervals

(useful in offices, canteens, warehouses, supermarkets and the like)

- *Timesheets*, filled in by individuals on a daily or weekly basis, are useful for work more easily measured by time spent than by output, but they rely heavily on individuals' truthfulness and conscientiousness

- *Computer recording,* as many jobs require the use of a PC and computer systems can be set up to record what individuals are doing (eg 'clocking-in' systems, which are a forerunner of this and are still widely used)

Bonus schemes

One reason for measuring work may be to reward performance.

- Piecework schemes pay higher rates for increased levels of output

- Individual or group bonus schemes can be devised according to any sort of formula that is acceptable to the employer and the employees

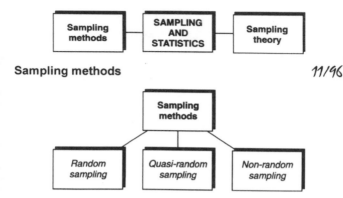

Not only is it impossible, it is also pointless to measure every work activity because sampling provides sufficiently reliable data at much lower cost.

Random sampling

● Every item in the population has an equal chance of being included in the sample

● Method

   ○ Construct a *sampling frame* (a numbered list of all items in the population)

   ○ Use random number tables or a computer to pick a sample from the sampling frame

Quasi-random sampling

These methods provide a good approximation to random sampling. A sampling frame is needed.

● Systematic sampling

- o Every nth item after a random start is selected
- o Ensure that there is no regular pattern in the population which, if it coincided with the *sampling interval*, might lead to a biased sample

- Stratified sampling
  - o The population is divided into strata or categories and a random sample is taken from each stratum, the number in each sample being proportional to the total in each stratum
  - o This is useful in situations that require many important categories to be covered by a relatively small overall sample
  - o Bias could arise because of the subjective nature of choosing the strata

- Multistage sampling
  - o The population is divided into smaller and smaller groups and a random sample of groups is taken at each stage of division
  - o This saves money but it is not truly random and there is a strong possibility of bias

Non-random sampling

These methods are used if a sampling frame does not exist.

- Quota sampling
  - o Sample each item until a certain quota is satisfied
  - o A large degree of bias can be introduced accidentally but can be partly overcome by subdividing the quota into different types inherent in the population

- Cluster sampling
  - This is similar to multistage sampling in that the population is divided into small groups, but *every* item in a random selection of small groups is examined
  - It is a good, inexpensive alternative to multistage sampling if no sampling frame exists
  - There is considerable potential for bias because of the non-random method of choosing clusters

Sampling theory   *5/95, 11/95, 11/96-11/99*

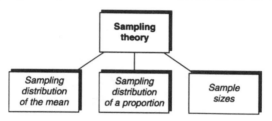

Sampling theory allows us to determine characteristics of a population by consideration of a sample taken from that population.

Sampling distribution of the mean

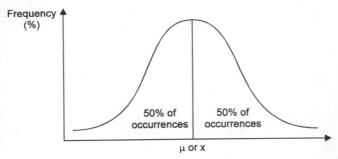

If a series of random samples (n > 30) is taken from a population and the mean of each sample is calculated, the resulting distribution (sampling distribution of the mean) has the following properties.

- It is very close to being normally distributed (*Central Limit Theorem*)

- Mean of sampling distribution = mean of population, μ

- Standard deviation of sampling distribution = standard error of the mean, se

- se = $\sigma/\sqrt{n}$ (where n is the size of each sample and σ is the standard deviation of the population)

- However σ is normally not known and so we use se = $s/\sqrt{n}$ (where s is the standard deviation of the sample)

With our knowledge of the above properties we can predict the following.

- There is a 68% probability that the population μ lies in the range 'sample mean ± 1 se'

- There is a 95% probability that μ lies in the range 'sample mean $\pm$ 1.96 se'

- There is a 99% probability that μ lies in the range 'sample mean $\pm$ 2.58 se'

'95%' is a *confidence level;* the range 'sample mean $\pm$ 2.58se' is a *confidence interval;* and the ends of the range 'sample mean $\pm$ 2.58se' are *confidence limits.*

Example: The average cost of doing a particular job has been derived from a sample of 169 jobs. The average is £1,300 with a standard deviation of £130.

Estimated confidence limits for the true average cost of doing the job at the 95% level of confidence

$$= £1,300 \pm £(1.96 \times 130/\sqrt{169})$$
$$= £1,300 \pm £19.60 = £1,280.40 \text{ to } £1,319.60$$

Sampling distribution of a proportion

This sampling distribution is normally distributed, has a mean equal to the population proportion and has a standard deviation equal to the standard error of a proportion = $\sqrt{(pq/n)}$ where p is the proportion in the population (the sample proportion is used as an estimate), q is $(1 - p)$ and n is the size of the sample.

Example: In a random sample of 500 out of 120,000 houses in a city, 100 had cable TV.

The sample proportion = 100/500 = 0.2, the standard error = $\sqrt{(0.2 (1 - 0.2)/500)} = 0.018$

An estimate of the proportion of houses with cable TV in the city at the 95% confidence level = the sample proportion ± 1.96 se

$$= 0.2 \pm (1.96 \times 0.018)$$
$$= 0.2 \pm 0.035$$

The percentage of houses with cable TV is between 16.5% and 23.5% at the 95% level of confidence.

Sample sizes

To determine the size of the sample needed in order to have a specific degree of accuracy at, say, the 95% level of confidence, we use the formulae

$$n \geq \left(\frac{1.96\sigma}{r} \right)^2 \text{ or } n \geq \frac{1.96^2 pq}{r^2}$$

where r is the degree of accuracy required in terms of units from the true mean. These formulae are *not* given in CIMA *Mathematical Tables*.

> *Exam focus.* All of the calculations described in the 'sampling theory' section of this chapter have already been examined, and you can expect them to feature regularly in future exams.

11/99

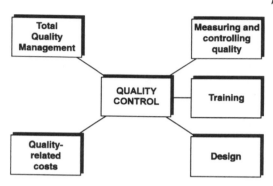

Total Quality Management   *11/98, 5/99*

Total Quality Management is the process of focusing on quality in the management of *all* resources and relationships within the organisation. There are two basic principles.

- *Getting things right first time*, on the basis that the cost of correcting mistakes is greater than the cost of preventing them from happening in the first place

- *Continuous improvement* - the belief that it is *always* possible to improve, no matter how high quality may be already

Measuring and controlling quality

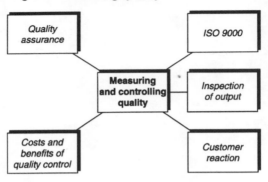

Quality assurance

The supplier guarantees the quality of goods supplied. This places the onus on the supplier to carry out the necessary quality checks or face cancellation of the contract.

ISO 9000

Suppliers may be required to obtain certification of their quality standards, for example under a quality assurance scheme such as ISO 9000 (formerly BS 5750).

ISO 9000 certification testifies that the organisation is operating to a structure of *written policies and procedures* which are designed to ensure it can consistently deliver a product or service to meet customer requirements.

Inspection of output

More emphasis is put upon 'in-process' controls such as statistical process controls and random sampling rather than waiting until the product is finally completed.

Statistical control charts can be established using sampling theory. They show the standard specification and upper and lower warning and action limits. See Chapter 9.

Customer reaction

Complaints in the following forms may be monitored.

- Letters
- Returned goods
- Penalty discounts incurred
- Claims under guarantee
- Requests for servicing of goods supplied

A more proactive approach is adopted in many organisations.

- Customer care plans
- After sales service
- Questionnaires

This is better than assuming that everything is all right if nobody complains.

Costs and benefits of quality control

Benefits include the following.

- Staying up with or ahead of the competition
- A good reputation with customers
- Cost savings (see later)
- Increased job satisfaction

Costs include the following.

- Costs of inspection of inputs (or premium prices under quality assurance schemes)

- Costs of redesigning products and methods and retraining employees

- Costs of monitoring customer feedback on outputs

Exam focus. The costs and benefits of quality control was the subject of a question in the Specimen paper. In the November 1995 paper candidates were asked how quality control could be improved in a hotel chain with no formal quality systems and a slightly complacent attitude: this was very much an *application* question rather than straight regurgitation of knowledge.

Training

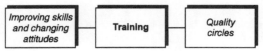

Improving skills and changing attitudes

Training for quality has two aspects.

- *Improving skills.* Workers are 'empowered' and encouraged to become multi-skilled

- *Changing attitudes.* Workers are encouraged to take responsibility for their work

Quality circles

Quality circles are groups of employees who meet regularly to discuss problems of quality in their area of work and suggest improvements.

Design

Quality should be designed into the following.

- The product itself (parts and materials used, user-friendliness etc)

- The production process

- Administrative and support processes

Quality-related costs

Quality costs

Make sure you can list and explain the different types of quality costs and be prepared to identify examples in given scenarios. The BS 6143 definitions are as follows.

- *Internal failure cost*: 'Costs arising within the organisation of failure to achieve the quality specified'

- *External failure cost*: 'Costs arising outside the manufacturing organisation of failure to achieve specified quality (after transfer of ownership to the customer)'

- *Appraisal cost*: 'The costs of assessing quality achieved'

- *Prevention cost*: 'The cost of any action taken to investigate, prevent or reduce defects and failures'

Quality savings

Savings may be made through quality management programmes in areas such as the following.

- Reduced materials purchases

- Reduced stores losses

- Reduced losses in process

- Reduced rejects/seconds

- Reduced machine running time

- Reduced idle time

- Reduced inspection costs

- Reduced administration costs

- Reduced returns from customers

- Reduced product liability claims

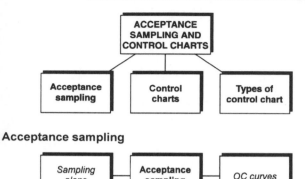

Acceptance sampling

Sampling plans — **Acceptance sampling** — *OC curves*

Sampling plans

Acceptance sampling has mainly been developed through the British Standards Institute, who provide ready-made *sampling plans* to help businesses work out how large a sample they should test to keep down the risk of accepting batches of supplies that were actually faulty.

With a *double sampling plan,* a second sample is tested if the first is not good enough to be acceptable but not bad enough to be unacceptable and the cumulative results are considered.

OC curves

Different plans have different *operating characteristics (OC)*. An OC curve can be drawn showing that if a delivery has x% defectives, the probability that it will be accepted using the plan is y%.

> *Exam focus*. Be aware of acceptance sampling and OC curves for the purposes of written questions. Numerical questions are very unlikely.

Control charts   5/96, 5/98

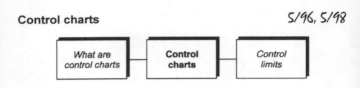

What are control charts?

Control charts allow managers to see trends at a glance and recognise when the operation being monitored should be stopped and corrected.

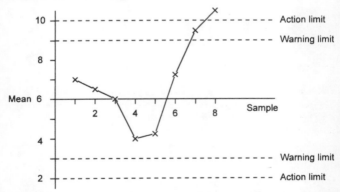

- The vertical axis shows the variable being measured - size, weight or whatever

- The horizontal axis starts at the mean size/weight/etc and shows the sample number

Control limits

- To all intents and purposes, 100% of all values in a normally distributed population will fall within ±3 standard errors of the mean

- If values outside this range are recorded the item must come from a different - faulty - population

- The upper and lower control limits (UCL/LCL to use CIMA *Mathematical Tables* terminology) are therefore *action* limits, at which something should be done to correct the process

- In reality the process should be stopped before it is completely out of control and so *warning* limits can be set as, say, 95% limits (± 1.96 standard errors)

Example: The mean is 10, the standard deviation of the population is 5 and the sample size is 150.

se = $\sigma / \sqrt{n}$ = 0.4

The action limits will be at 10 ± 3 × 0.4 = 8.8 and 11.2

The warning limits will be at 10 ± 1.96 × 0.4 = 9.2 and 10.8

Exam focus. Don't forget that CIMA *Mathematical Tables* provides information about control limits.

Types of control chart   5/96

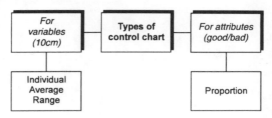

For variables (10 cm)

Control charts may be drawn for the following.

- *Individual units*: one unit may be taken at random at regular intervals and measured

- *Averages ($\bar{x}$ charts)*: a number of units are taken and measured at regular intervals and the mean of each batch ($\bar{x}$) is then plotted on the control chart

- *Ranges ($\bar{R}$ charts)*: an $\bar{x}$ chart involves a lot of work but a simpler method is as follows

  o Take small random samples of a constant size and calculate the range (highest minus lowest measurement)

  o Calculate and plot the mean of these ranges ($\bar{R}$)

  o Given a target for the mean, T, the control limits are set at $T \pm A\bar{R}$, where A is read from statistical process control tables

For attributes (good/bad)

- If what is being measured is an *attribute* (good/bad) as opposed to a variable (size, weight), the item will either pass or not pass the test

- In this case regular samples are taken and the *proportion* of faulty items is calculated

- The proportions are plotted on a control chart (a *p chart*)

- The control limits are calculated as for confidence limits for a proportion (see Chapter 7)

- The control chart looks like this

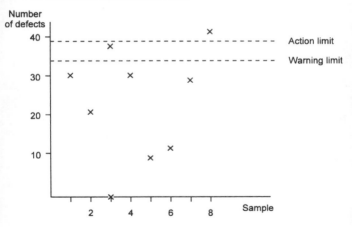

- o Number of faulty items is shown on the horizontal axis
- o The horizontal axis is drawn from 0 and shows the sample number
- o Lower limits can be calculated and drawn, but since the ideal is as few defects as possible, this would only

be appropriate if a certain number of defects was inevitable and a lower number indicated that the sampling process was going wrong (action: investigate and correct sampling procedures)

Exam focus. In the latest Guidance Notes to be issued by the CIMA it states that 'only an awareness of r charts is required.' The examiner has confirmed that calculations involving r charts will not be required.

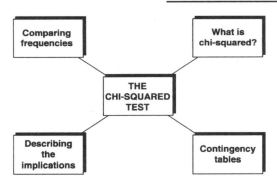

Comparing frequencies
5/95, 11/95, 11/96, 5/97, 11/97, 11/98, 5/99

As seen in Chapter 7, significance testing using the *normal* distribution compares *means*. Significance testing using the *chi-squared distribution* compares *frequencies*.

For example, a claim that nine out of ten dogs prefer X dog food might be tested on three samples of 100 dogs with the following results.

	Sample 1	*Sample 2*	*Sample 3*
Prefer X	88	70	10
Prefer other food	12	30	90
	100	100	100

Each result can be compared with the expected result.

	Observed O	Expected E	O-E	$(O-E)^2$	$(O-E)^2/E$
Sample 1					
Prefer X	88	90	-2	4	0.04
Prefer other	12	10	2	4	0.40
Sample 2					
Prefer X	70	90	-20	400	4.44
Prefer other	30	10	20	400	40.00
Sample 3					
Prefer X	10	90	-80	6,400	71.11
Prefer other	90	10	80	6,400	640.00

- The expected frequency in each case is 90 dogs in the 'prefer X' category and 10 in the 'prefer other' category

- The extent to which the *observed sample frequencies* conform to the *expected frequencies* is measured by the figures in the $(O-E)^2/E$ column
  - The smaller the figure in the $(O-E)^2/E$ column, the smaller the difference between observed and expected results
  - If the figure were 0 there would be no difference
  - When 88 dogs prefer X this is very close to the expected figure so $(O-E)^2/E$ is only 0.04
  - When 90 dogs 'prefer other' this is very different from the expected result, so $(O-E)^2/E$ is much higher (640)

Exam focus. Students often learn the mechanics of a technique without having the slightest idea of what they are really doing. They are then stuck when they are asked to explain or interpret their calculations. The above example has deliberately been made simple enough for you to be able to deduce the results without doing any calculations. How do the figures calculated confirm what you would deduce about each sample in any case?

What is chi-squared?

5/95, 11/95, 11/96, 5/97, 11/97, 11/98, 5/99

- The chi-squared *statistic* is what you calculate
  - It is the sum of the figures in the $(O-E)^2/E$ column
  - CIMA *Mathematical Tables* tell you that:

  $$\chi^2 = \Sigma \frac{(O-E)^2}{E}$$

  - In the dog food example, χ^2 is 755.99

- Chi-squared distribution tables give a series of 'critical values'
  - These are points *above which* it is likely that there is a significant difference between observed and expected frequencies
  - To put it another way, if there is a significant difference between observed and expected frequencies, tables show the critical values (at various levels of probability) that *would be exceeded* by the value you calculate
  - If you are testing at the '99% level of confidence' you want only a 1% probability that your calculated χ^2 exceeds the critical table value, so you use the column labelled 1

Exam focus. Chi-squared questions set so far have not specified a confidence level, and the calculated value has had to be assessed at the full range of probabilities (you might say '... there is no significant difference at any level of confidence ...') by reading across the relevant row.

- The rows in the chi-squared distribution tables represent different *degrees of freedom* which, for the type of chi-squared test that is likely to appear in the MSA exam, are calculated by reference to the rows and columns of 'contingency tables'

Contingency tables

5/95, 11/95, 11/96, 5/97, 11/97, 5/98, 5/99

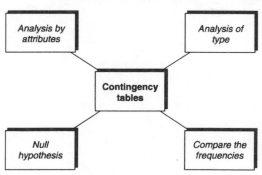

Analysis by attributes

A contingency table sets out data that shows the association or correspondence between two or more *attributes*.

- Attributes might be things like spending habits, size of order, holiday preferences (examples from MSA exams) or similar

- Typically a business will be examining information about its customers to try to improve marketing and targeting of products

Analysis by type

A contingency table also analyses the data according to types. Types might be things like 'local or 'non-local', 'retailers' or 'wholesalers', different age-groups or the like.

> *Exam focus.* If you are confused about what is an 'attribute' and what is a 'type', a strong clue in MSA exams is the word 'type'!

Here is the sort of data you might be given.

	Attribute			
Type	*A*	*B*	*C*	*Totals*
x	a	b	c	X
y	aa	bb	cc	Y
z	aaa	bbb	ccc	Z
	A	B	C	T

Here is the *contingency table* derived from this. The letters show how the figures correspond.

	Attribute A		*Attribute B*		*Attribute C*	
Type	*Observed*	*Expected*	*Observed*	*Expected*	*Observed*	*Expected*
x	a	A/T × X	b	B/T × X	c	C/T × X
y	aa	A/T × Y	bb	B/T × Y	cc	C/T × Y
z	aaa	A/T × Z	bbb	B/T × Z	ccc	C/T × Z
	A	A	B	B	C	C

Note that this table has three rows of types and three columns of attributes.

- Transfer the data in the question into the 'observed' columns, and sum them (figures A, B and C)

- Find the overall total number of *types* (T), and the total of individual types (X, Y and Z)

- The expected number of type x's with attribute A is the observed percentage with attribute A (A/T%) times the observed total of types x (X) (ie A/T × X)

- Perform this calculation for each figure in the expected columns

Compare the frequencies

The next step is to *compare the frequencies*, as follows.

	O	E	(O-E)	(O-E)^2	(O-E)^2/E
Attribute A					
Type x					
Type y	As above			Calculated figures	
Type z					
Attribute B					
Type x					
etc					

Calculated $\overline{\chi^2}$

The number of *degrees of freedom* is calculated as

(rows − 1) × (columns − 1)

Here it is $(3 − 1)(3 − 1) = 4$

The calculated χ^2 can then be compared with the critical value shown in the relevant row of the chi-squared distribution tables at various levels of confidence.

Null hypothesis

It is usual to establish a *null hypothesis*. A null hypothesis states that there is no significant difference between observed and expected frequencies.

The null hypothesis is proved true if:

calculated chi-squared value ≤ critical chi-squared value

Describing the implications

5/95, 11/95, 11/96, 5/97, 11/97

Questions will ask you to describe the implications of your chi-squared calculations.

- The null hypothesis may be true

    o For example, there may be no significant difference between spending habits of local and non-local customers

    o This might indicate that there is no advantage in, say, providing special facilities like car parks or crèches to encourage non-local customers

- The null hypothesis may be false

    o For example, holiday preferences may be significantly different depending on age-group and this would indicate that different holidays should be more closely tailored to and targeted at different groups

    o The $(O-E)^2/E$ column should be examined to see in which types the most significant differences (the largest figures) occur, and comments made as appropriate

---

Exam focus. The chi-squared test has made frequent appearances in the current syllabus MSA exams. Maybe it is time for a rest, but make sure you can do the calculations and interpret them just in case.

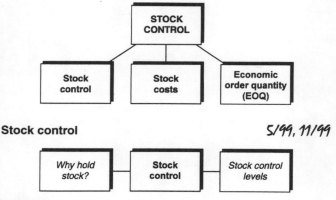

Stock control   *5/99, 11/99*

Why hold stock?

- To ensure goods are available to meet expected demand

- To meet any future shortages

- To take advantage of bulk purchasing discounts

- To absorb seasonal fluctuations and any variations in usage and demand (capacity management?)

- To allow production processes to flow smoothly and efficiently

- As a necessary part of the production process

- As a deliberate investment policy

Stock control levels

- Reorder level = maximum usage × maximum lead time

- Reorder quantity

- Minimum level = reorder level − (average usage × average lead time)

- Maximum level = reorder level + reorder quantity − (minimum usage × minimum lead time)

Stock costs   5/95, 5/96, 5/97

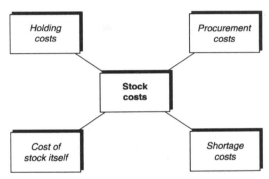

- If huge stocks are built up *holding costs* will be incurred unnecessarily

- On the other hand, if stocks are kept low, small quantities of stock will have to be ordered more frequently, thereby increasing *ordering costs*

- *Stockout costs* may also arise if stocks are kept too low

Holding costs

- Cost of capital tied up
- Warehousing and handling costs
- Deterioration and obsolescence
- Insurance

- Pilferage

Procurement costs

- Ordering costs (clerical costs, receiving goods into store) if goods are obtained from outside suppliers

- Production set-up costs if goods are manufactured internally
  - The cost of lost production while the production run is being set up
  - Variable costs associated with production planning and preparing the labour force and machinery for a production run

Shortage costs

- The loss of a sale and the contribution from the sale

- The extra cost of buying an emergency supply of stocks at a higher cost

- The cost of lost production and sales if a stockout brings an entire process to a halt

Cost of stock itself

- The supplier's price or the direct cost per unit of production

- This is especially important if there are bulk purchase discounts/savings in direct production costs on longer production runs

Total costs are minimised when holding costs per time period and ordering costs per time period are equal.

> *Exam focus*. There were 6 marks available in the May 1998 exam
> for describing the basic principles of stock control policy and
> explaining why a good stock control policy would be of value to
> the company described in the scenario.

Economic order quantity (EOQ)
5/95, 5/96, 11/96, 5/97, 5/98, 5/99, 11/99

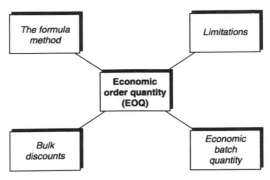

EOQ is the quantity to purchase to ensure that holding costs
and ordering costs are kept to a minimum.

The formula method

$$Q = \sqrt{\frac{2C_oD}{C_h}}$$

where   D = usage in units per time period
             (demand)

         Co = cost of making one order

         Ch = holding cost per unit of stock per
              time period

         Q = quantity ordered

For example, the demand for a commodity is 40,000 units a year at a steady rate. It costs £20 to place an order, and 40p to hold a unit for a year.

- EOQ = $\sqrt{\dfrac{2CoD}{Ch}}$ = $\sqrt{\dfrac{2 \times 20 \times 40,000}{0.4}}$ = 2,000 units

- Orders placed each year = $\dfrac{40,000}{2,000}$ = 20

- Frequency of orders = 52 weeks/20 orders = every 2.6 weeks

Limitations

The EOQ model is based on a number of assumptions.

- Demand is certain, constant and continuous over time
- Supply lead time is constant
- Customers' orders cannot be held while fresh stocks are awaited
- No stockouts are permitted
- All prices are constant and certain, there being no bulk purchase discounts
- The cost of holding stock is proportional to the quantity of stock held

Economic batch quantity   5/98

Where there is gradual re-supply of stocks the formula is modified to

$$Q = \sqrt{\dfrac{2CoD}{Ch(1 - D/R)}}$$

where R = the production rate (or supply rate) of the items of stock per time period.

> *Exam focus.* Students often confuse D and R in the EBQ formula. D is an organisation's demand for the item whereas R is the maximum rate at which the item can be made or replenished.

Bulk discounts

Total costs will be minimised at one of the following points.

- The pre-discount EOQ level (so that a discount is not worthwhile)

- At the minimum order size necessary to earn the discount

The technique, therefore, is to calculate the EOQ both with and without discounts and then calculate the total annual (or monthly/weekly etc, as appropriate) costs. Choose the cheapest option.

> *Exam focus.* In the November 1996 exam, candidates were required to apply stock control theory to a system of bank accounts. In the November 1999 exam candidates were once again required to apply stock control theory, this time to the tyre division of a chain of garages. These questions may sound difficult but they weren't too complicated as candidates were actually told to use a stock control system. Be prepared for unusual applications of straightforward techniques.

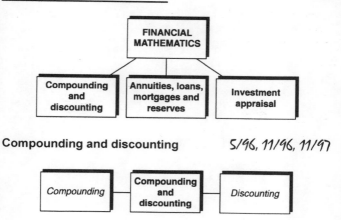

Compounding and discounting *5/96, 11/96, 11/97*

Compounding

As interest is earned, it is added to the original investment and earns interest itself.

The formula is $V = X(1 + r)^n$

Example: £100 for 3 years at 10% = £100 × $(1.1)^3$ = £133.10

(In its negative form, $V = X(1 - r)^n$, the formula can be used in situations involving *depreciation* by the reducing balance method. V is the residual value and X the original value.)

Discounting

Discounting is the reverse of compounding. It involves determining the equivalent worth today (*present value*) of a future cash flow.

The formula is X(the PV) = $V × 1/(1+r)^n$

Example: £133.10 received in year three has a present value (at 10%) of £133.10 × $1/(1.1)^3$ = £100.

Discount factors are shown in present value tables provided in the exam, or they can be calculated as $1/(1 + r)^n$.

Annuities, loans, mortgages and reserves
                                    5/95, 11/95, 11/96, 11/97, 5/98

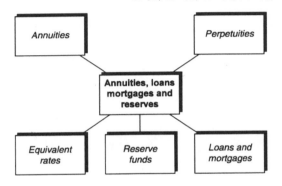

Annuities

An *annuity* is a constant sum of money each year for a given number of years. The PV of an annuity is found using one of the following methods.

- Multiply the annuity by the relevant cumulative present value factor read from CIMA *Mathematical Tables*

- If tables do not show the relevant rate or number of years, calculate the factor using the formula below and then multiply the annuity by it

Annuity factor $= \dfrac{1}{r} - \dfrac{1}{r(1+r)^t}$

Example: the PV of £50 pa for two years at 10.5% is

$$\text{£50} \times \left(\frac{1}{0.105} - \frac{1}{0.105(1.105)^2} \right) = \text{£50} \times 1.724 = \text{£86.20}$$

Exam focus. For too long management accounting exams have presented students with unrealistically simplified scenarios, such as 'interest rates are 10%'. In real life interest rates are usually something like '7.35%' or '11.029%' and business decisions cover periods longer than the 15 years shown in CIMA *Mathematical Tables*. The MSA examiner is keen that students understand the principles so that they can use them in real life. Be prepared for this in your exam.

Perpetuities

- The present value of an annuity which lasts for ever is the annuity divided by r

- £100 per annum for ever at 10% has a PV of £1,000 (it is just like having £1,000 capital and earning 10% interest (£100) on it every year)

Loans and mortgages

A *loan* is often repaid in regular periodic instalments. A *mortgage* is simply a secured loan. The amount to repay is

$$\frac{\text{Loan}}{\text{Annuity factor}}$$

Example: for a car loan of £2,000 at 10.5% to be repaid in two annual instalments the annual repayment is £2,000/1.724 = £1,160.09. (For the annuity factor, see above.)

Reserve funds

To build up a sum in the future by regular savings, proceed as follows.

* Work out the PV of the future sum: multiply by $1/(1 + r)^n$ (ie divide by $(1 + r)^n$)

* Work out the annuity factor, or look it up if possible

* Divide the PV by the annuity factor, the result being the amount that needs to be saved each period

Example: to have £3,000 in 3 year's time if r = 10% you need to save:

$$\frac{£3,000 \times 1/(1+r)^n}{\dfrac{1}{r} - \dfrac{1}{r(1+r)^t}} = \frac{3,000 \times 0.751}{2.487} = £905.91$$

(*Note*. The n and the t are the same thing here, but we stick to the formulae as given in CIMA *Mathematical Tables*. If you work this out on your calculator without rounding you get £906.34.)

The advantage of a reserve fund is that you don't owe money or have to pay interest when you want to use it to invest in new assets.

The disadvantages are that you have to wait, and you can't use the money for anything else.

Equivalent rates

Domestic mortgages and some other loans are usually repaid on a monthly basis. This does not affect the techniques already described: you simply need to be able to calculate rates per period rather than rates per year, or *vice versa*.

- 10% per annum = $(1.1^{1/12} - 1)\%$ = 0.797% per month

- 0.797% per month = $1.00797^{12} - 1$ = 10%

These formulae are *not* given in CIMA *Mathematical Tables*.

Investment appraisal
5/95, 5/96, 11/96, 5/97, 5/98, 11/98, 5/99, 11/99

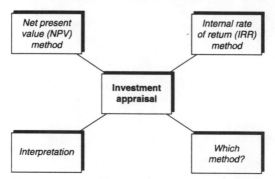

Discounted cash flow (DCF) techniques can be applied to the cash flows associated with an investment to ascertain whether the investment is worth undertaking.

Net present value (NPV) method

- Work out present values of all cash flows (income and expenditure) related to an investment

- Work out a net total (NPV)
  - Positive NPV - investment acceptable
  - Negative NPV - investment unacceptable

- If two or more projects are viable they can be ranked in order of highest NPV per pound invested (NPV/investment)

- Cash flows spread over a year are assumed to occur at the year end

- 'Now' is the last day of year 0

- Here is the layout, with easy figures for illustration

Year	Cash flow	Discount factor	Present value
	£	10%	£
0	10,000	1.000	10,000
1	1,000	0.909	909
2 - 4*	10,000	2.261	22,610
		NPV	33,519

* The discount factor is the cumulative year 4 factor minus the cumulative year 1 factor (or the sum of the single period factors for years 2 to 4), but do years 2, 3 and 4 separately if you are worried about this

---

Exam focus. If an examination question asks you to calculate the constant annual revenue a machine needs to earn to ensure that it breaks even, this will simply involve determining a constant cash inflow (say R) over the life of the machine (n years) such that the NPV of the inflows (= R × cumulative discount factor at r% for n years) = NPV of costs.

Annualised equivalents enable you to compare the NPVs of projects with different durations.

- An annualised equivalent is an equivalent constant cash flow (an annuity) in present value terms of a series of irregular cash flows

- Calculated as $\dfrac{\text{NPV of project}}{\text{Cumulative PV factor for life of project}}$

Internal rate of return (IRR) method

- IRR = investment's rate of return = rate of interest at which NPV is 0

- To determine the IRR of a one- or two-year investment, equate the PV of costs with the PV of benefits

- To determine the IRR of a more lengthy investment, use *interpolation*

  o Calculate the NPV using a rough estimate of the IRR

    - If the NPV is negative, recalculate the NPV using a lower rate

    - If the NPV is positive, recalculate the NPV using a higher rate

- Calculate the IRR either by plotting the points on a graph or by using $a\% + [\dfrac{A}{A-B} \times (b-a)]\%$ where

  a = one interest rate
  b = the other interest rate
  A = NPV at rate a
  B = NPV at rate b

Which method?

NPV is a superior decision tool, because IRR ignores the relative size of investments and cannot be used to select between mutually exclusive projects.

Interpretation

Possible problems you might mention when asked to interpret your results are the uncertainty of future cash flows, the possibly arbitrary choice of a discount rate and difficulties in obtaining the funds to invest in the first place.

Exam focus. The May 1997 exam contained a question that required candidates to calculate five different NPVs, convert them into annualised equivalents and *then* to explain their answers in non-technical English for the benefit of a non-numerate manager. You *must* make sure that you understand all of the MSA syllabus topics well enough to be able to explain them when required to do so in the written parts of exam questions.

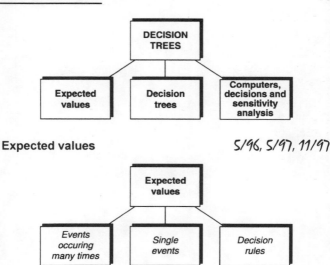

Expected values   *5/96, 5/97, 11/97*

The expected outcome of an event/several events is called the expected value (EV). If the probability of an outcome is p, then the expected number of times that this outcome will occur in n events (the EV) = n × p.

For example, the probability that a component is defective is 0.04. The number of defective components expected in a batch of 2,000 = EV = 2,000 × 0.04 = 80.

Events occurring many times

If an event occurs many times then, in the long run, the expected value should be approximately the actual average.

For example, the daily sales of product X may be as follows.

Units	Probability	EV
50	0.1	5
60	0.8	48
70	0.1	7
	1.0	60

In the long run the actual average daily sales of product X should be 60 units.

Single events

An expected value can be calculated when an event will only occur once or twice, but it will not be a true long-run average of what will actually happen because there is no long run.

For example, a project has three possible outcomes.

Profit/loss	Probability	EV
£		
40,000	0.1	4,000
7,000	0.7	4,900
(5,000)	0.2	(1,000)
		7,900

Decision rules

In the example above, a profit of £7,900 will not occur but the expected value can be used to help management decide whether or not to invest in a project.

- Positive EV (ie EV is a profit), accept project
- Negative EV (ie EV is a loss), reject project

An alternative decision rule is the choice of the option or alternative which has the highest EV of profit (or the lowest EV of cost).

> *Exam focus*. Commentary on EV decisions or decision tree decisions should draw attention to the fact that the probabilities and cash flows are estimates.

Decision trees   *11/95, 5/96, 5/97, 11/97, 5/99, 11/99*

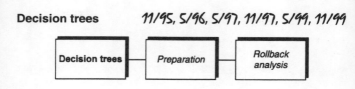

Preparation

- Start with a (labelled) *decision point*

- Add branches for each option/alternative

- If the outcome of an option is 100% certain, the branch for that alternative is complete

- If the outcome of an option is uncertain (ie there are a number of possible outcomes), add a (labelled) *outcome point*

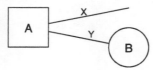

- For each possible outcome, a branch (with the relevant probability) should be added to the outcome point

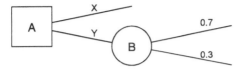

- Always label the branches with a word or phrase and each decision point and outcome point with a letter

- Always work *chronologically* from left to right

Rollback analysis

Rollback analysis is the technique used to evaluate a decision with a decision tree. Working from *right to left*, the EV of revenue/cost/contribution/profit is calculated at each *outcome point*.

For example, as a result of an increase in demand for a town's car parking facilities, the owners of a car park are reviewing their business operations. A decision has to be made now to select one of the following three options for the next year.

Option 1: Make no change. Annual profit is £100,000. There is little likelihood that this will provoke new competition this year.

Option 2: Raise prices by 50%. If this occurs there is a 75% chance that an entrepreneur will set up in competition this year. The Board's estimate of its annual profit in this situation would be as follows.

	2A WITH a new competitor		2B WITHOUT a new competitor	
Probability		Profit £	Probability	Profit £
0.3		150,000	0.7	200,000
0.7		120,000	0.3	150,000

Option 3: Expand the car park quickly, at a cost of £50,000, keeping prices the same. The profits are then estimated to be like 2B above, except that the probabilities would be 0.6 and 0.4 respectively

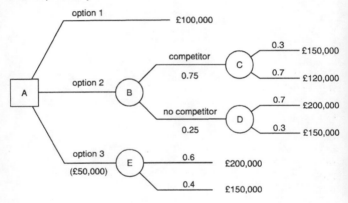

At C, expected profit = (150 × 0.3) + (120 × 0.7) = £129,000

At D, expected profit = (200 × 0.7) + (150 x 0.3) = £185,000

At B, expected profit = (129 × 0.75) + (185 × 0.25) = £143,000

At E, expected profit = (200 × 0.6) + (150 × 0.4) = £180,000

Option	Expected profit £'000
1	100
2	143
3 (180 – 50)	130

Option 2 has the highest EV of profit so this is the one to choose.

Exam focus. When decision trees have been examined in recent sittings, there have generally been 10 marks available for drawing the tree, and a further 15 marks for analysis, recommendations and limitations of the tree. Remember to draw diagrams neatly, with a sharp pencil and ruler and to label the decision points and branches clearly. Make sure that you are able to answer the discursive parts of the question as well - these are usually straightforward and should not be omitted.

Computers, decisions and sensitivity analysis   5/96

Spreadsheets are ideally suited to sensitivity analysis. By setting up a mathematical model of the problem and using 'data tables' or 'what if' macros/'scenarios', it is possible to evaluate a wide range of possible outcomes, changing the variables at the touch of a button.

Exam focus. You will not have to devise spreadsheets in the exam or have knowledge of any particular spreadsheet package but you may have to *explain* have a spreadsheet can be used to aid decision making, as in the May 1996 exam.

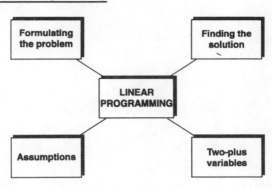

Linear programming is a technique for allocating scarce resources so as to maximise profit or minimise costs.

For example, suppose a company makes two products. Relevant data are as follows.

	Standard	Deluxe	Availability per month
Profit per unit	£15	£20	
Labour hours per unit	5	10	4,000
Kgs of material per unit	10	5	4,250

Find the production plan which will maximise profit.

Formulating the problem

5/95, 5/96, 11/96, 5/98, 11/98, 11/99

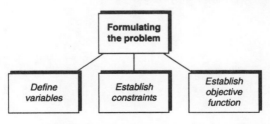

Define variables

- Let x = number of standard produced each month

- Let y = number of deluxe produced each month

Establish constraints

- Labour : $5x + 10y \leq 4,000$

- Material: $10x + 5y \leq 4,250$

- Non negativity: $x \geq 0$, $y \geq 0$

Establish objective function

- Profit $(P) = 15x + 20y$

Exam focus. Students often have problems with constraints of the style 'the quantity of one type must not exceed twice that of the other'. This can be interpreted as follows: the quantity of one type (say X) must not exceed (must be less than or equal to) twice that of the other (2Y) (i.e. $X \leq 2Y$).

Finding the solution   *5/96, 11/96, 5/98, 11/98, 11/99*

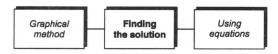

Graphical method

- Graph the constraints

  - Labour: $5x + 10y = 4,000$; if $x = 0$, $y = 400$ and if $y = 0$, $x = 800$

  - Material: $10x + 5y = 4,250$; if $x = 0$, $y = 850$ and if $y = 0$, $x = 425$

- Establish the *feasible area/region*, which is the area where *all* inequalities are satisfied (area above x axis and y axis ($x \geq 0$, $y \geq 0$), below material constraint ($\leq$) *and* below labour constraint ($\leq$))

> *Exam focus.* There were six marks available in the November 1999 exam for drawing a suitable graph for a linear programming problem and shading the feasible region (there was no requirement to solve the linear programming problem).

- Add an iso-profit line (suppose P = £3,000 so that if P = 15x + 20y then if x = 0, y = 150 and if y = 0, x = 200) and (sliding your ruler across the page if necessary) find the point furthest from the origin but still in the feasible area

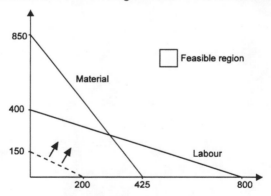

- Use simultaneous equations to find the x and y coordinates at the optimal solution, the intersection of the material and labour constraints (x = 300, y = 250)

If the objective were to minimise costs the optimal solution would be at the point in the feasible area closest to the origin.

> *Exam focus.* The May 1995 paper set a problem where the iso-profit line was exactly parallel to one of the constraint lines. This meant that there was no single optimum solution, but a *range* of solutions along the part of the line within the feasible area. Likewise, in the November 1996 exam there were a number of optimal solutions (points with integer co-ordinates along a line forming one boundary of the feasible area).

Using equations

- Graph the constraints and establish the feasible area/region as in the geographical method.

- Determine all possible intersection points of constraints and axes using simultaneous equations

- Calculate profit at each intersection point to determine which is the optimal solution

Two-plus variables   *11/99*

When there are more than two decision variables the graphical method cannot be used. Other methods are available but you do not need to know the details.

- The constraints are formulated as before except that an extra variable (a, b, c or whatever) called the *slack variable* is introduced to represent unused resources

- In a final simplex tableau we have the following
  - A solution *column* showing the value of each variable in the optimum solution
  - A solution *row* giving the *shadow price* of each variable
    - This is the opportunity cost of the scarce resource
    - It is the premium that it is worth paying to get an extra unit of the scarce resource

    – It shows how much the value of the objective function will change if the availability of the scarce resource changes by one unit

Computer tools such as Solver are preferable to simplex because they are easier and quicker to use.

Assumptions   *5/96, 11/96*

* All relationships are linear

* Partial units can be produced

* Products are independent of each other

* Costs, revenue and quantities available are known with certainty

* There is only one objective

Exam focus. Linear programming is one of the most commonly examined topics and you must be able to determine the optimal solution graphically *and* using simultaneous equations. If you have to draw a graph make sure that it has a title, that the axes are labelled and that the constraint lines and the feasible area are clearly identified. For two-plus variables you only need to know how to formulate the problem and interpret a given solution. You will not be tested on specific computer packages.

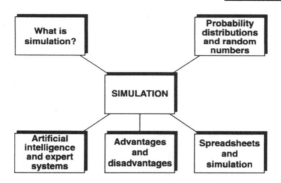

What is simulation?

- Simulation means building a model that imitates real-world conditions

- Relationships between variables are represented by mathematical formulae

- The EOQ model (see Chapter 11) is a simple simulation model

- The *Monte Carlo* method of simulation is used for the study of a dynamic system over time

  o In a dynamic system both the values of variables and the relationships between them change

  o The UK economy is a dynamic system

  o The market for a company's products is a dynamic system

- In operations management, simulation can be applied to problems like budget forecasts, queues at supermarket checkouts and so on

> *Exam focus.* Simulation was examined for the first time in November 1997. In addition to preparing a simulation, the question required candidates to comment on the results obtained and also to explain the use of computers and simulation. Simulation was examined again in May 1998 when candidates were required to simulate machine breakdowns and repair times using random number tables.

Probability distributions and random numbers

11/97, 5/98, 5/99

The construction of a simulation model entails the following.

- Defining the relationships between variables as formulae

- Identifying probability distributions for variables

- Allocating a range of numbers to each possible value

- Generating random numbers to assign actual values to the variables

To take a very simple example, suppose Lisa may receive one, two or three customer enquiries every five minutes. Probabilities are determined and ranges of random numbers allocated as follows.

Enquiries	Probability	Random number range
1	0.1	0
2	0.6	1 - 6
3	0.3	7 - 9

If a lucky dip then generates the random numbers 4, 8, 1, 0, 9, 3, the model would simulate the following pattern of calls.

Time	Random number	Enquiries
9.00 - 9.05	4	2
9.06 - 9.10	8	3
9.11 - 9.15	1	2
9.16 - 9.20	0	1
9.21 - 9.25	9	3
9.26 - 9.30	3	2
		13

In practice simulation models are complicated enough to justify extensive use of computers.

Spreadsheets and simulation   *5/96, 5/98*

Spreadsheet packages can help with simulations. Models can be designed, built and tested in a very short time and modern packages can be made to do sophisticated things, even by users with no programming knowledge.

There are limitations to their use, however.

- One-off problems may not justify the investment of time

- The model may be corrupted accidentally

- For complicated situations it may be difficult for the average user to define the necessary logic

Advantages and disadvantages

Advantages are as follows.

- Simulation provides a means of considering problems where other methods are not suitable

- It gives a better idea of the possible variations in outcome than 'ordinary' probability analysis and EV calculations

- Fewer simplifying assumptions are made than with other methods

- It is cheaper and quicker than experimenting with the real system, and it allows more or different scenarios to be tested than might happen to occur in a real-life test

Disadvantages are as follows.

- It is difficult to define all the relationships in suitable form

- There is a chance that the best solution will not be generated, or not spotted even if it is: simulation is not an optimising technique

Artificial intelligence and expert systems

Artificial intelligence is the study of how to make computers do things which, at the moment, people are better at doing (eg learning from experience and understanding other people's behaviour).

Artificial intelligence software works by creating a knowledge base that consists of facts, concepts and the relationships between them and then searches it using pattern-matching techniques to 'solve' problems.

Expert systems are the main commercial application of artificial intelligence.

- They are computer programs that allow users to benefit from expert knowledge and information

- The system consists of a database holding specialised data and rules about what to do in, or how to interpret, a given set of circumstances

- Applications include processing straightforward loan applications and legal and tax advice

Advantages include the following.

- The expertise is permanent (human experts leave the business)

- It can be copied easily

- It is consistent

- It can be documented

- Computers can be much faster than human beings

There are severe limitations, however.

- Systems are expensive

- The technology is still in its infancy

- Development is difficult and extensive testing and debugging is required

- People are *naturally* more creative

- Systems have a narrow focus

- People will resist being replaced by computers

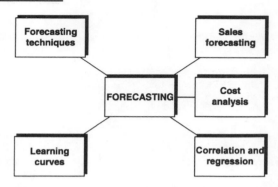

Forecasting techniques

5/96, 11/96, 11/98, 5/99

Forecasting is necessary for budgeting and longer-term planning.

- The Delphi method involves asking experts and finding a consensus

- Econometrics is the study of economic variables using computer models

- A variety of mathematical techniques exist for extrapolating historical data

---

Exam focus. Qualitative forecasting methods, such as the Delphi method, were the topic of a question in the November 1996 exam.

Sales forecasting

5/95, 5/97, 11/97, 11/99

Time series analysis

The moving averages technique (centring and taking averages) can be used to establish trends and seasonal variations.

- The *additive* model suggests that the actual figures comprise three components: *Trend + Seasonal + Random*

- If the elements are not independent the *multiplicative* model is preferable: *Trend × Seasonal × Random*

Exam focus. The May 1995 exam required you to find the trend over a certain number of quarters and then establish a growth rate per quarter. For example, if the trend changes from 100 to 125 over six quarters the growth rate is 125/100 = 1.25 or 25% over the whole period and $1.25^{1/6} = 1.0379$ or around 3.8% per quarter. (See Chapters 12 - 13 for equivalent interest rates.)

Exponential smoothing

The CIMA *Mathematical Tables* give the formula for this technique.

New Forecast = Old Forecast + A (old Actual Sales − Old Forecast), where A is a given smoothing factor.

Every new forecast reflects actual results in the past. This may not be appropriate, especially in a fast-changing modern environment.

Exam focus. Exponential smoothing was examined for the first time in November 1997.

Cost analysis   *11/99*

The high-low method is one method of dividing semi-variable costs.

- Review records of costs in previous periods and select the period with the highest activity level and the period with the lowest activity level

- If necessary, adjust costs to the same price level by means of a price index

- Total cost of high activity level minus total cost of low activity level = variable cost of difference in activity levels

- Determine the fixed cost by substitution

- For example, suppose the highest activity level is 10,000 units at a cost of £4,000 and the lowest 2,000 units at a cost of £1,600

  Variable cost = £(4,000 – 1,600)/(10,000 – 2,000) = £2,400/8,000 = 30p per unit

  ∴ Fixed cost = (using high level figures) £(4,000 – (10,000 × 0.3)) = £1,000

Correlation and regression *11/95, 5/96, 11/97-11/98, 11/99*

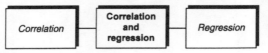

Correlation

The correlation between two variables can be measured by the *correlation coefficient*, *r*. The formula is given in CIMA *Mathematical Tables*.

$$r = \frac{n \sum XY - \sum X \sum Y}{\sqrt{[n \sum X^2 - (\sum X)^2][n \sum Y^2 - (\sum Y)^2]}}$$

- Positive correlation means that as X increases so does Y (eg output and costs)

- Negative correlation means that as X increases, Y decreases (eg prices and demand)

The *coefficient of determination*, r^2, measures the total variation in one variable that can be explained by variations in the other variable. If r = 0.8, r^2 = 0.64 which means that 64% of variations in Y can be explained by variations in X (not necessarily that they are *caused* by variations in X).

Regression

To predict values for one variable (Y) given values for the other (X) an equation is needed. The equation can be found by means of linear regression analysis.

- Linear regression analysis is used to derive a linear cost function Y = a + bX where

  Y is the dependent variable

  X is the independent variable

  a is fixed costs

  b is the variable cost per unit

  o For example, Y might be the total machine cost of a product and X might be running hours

  o To find a and b, the formulae to use are

  $$b = \frac{n\Sigma XY - \Sigma X\Sigma Y}{n\Sigma X^2 - (\Sigma X)^2} \quad \text{and} \quad a = \frac{\Sigma Y}{n} - \frac{b\Sigma X}{n}$$

  where n is the number of pairs of data for X and Y

  (*Note*. The formula for a is given in the form

  a = $\overline{Y}$ − b$\overline{X}$ (which is the same thing) in CIMA *Mathematical Tables*)

- Regression analysis can be used in conjunction with a time series (eg Month 1 - 10,000 units, Month 2 - 12,000 units, Month 3 - 14,000 units)

  o Let X = time, Y = units

  o Set the middle period = 0 (M1 = –1, M2 = 0, M3 = +1)

  o Calculate a and b as usual

  The figure you calculate for a will then be equal to average sales in the period (here 12,000 units). Can you see that the regression line equation is Y = 12,000 + 2,000 X?

Exam focus. The November 1995 exam included a question that gave you all the values for $\sum X$, $\sum X^2$ etc and simply required you to plug them into the formula. However, it then expected you to be able to *interpret* your answer.

- Because linear regression can be used to find the relationship between any two things, not just fixed and variable costs, you might derive the equation

  Y = 400 + 0.5X

  o If Y is, say, total costs, this would mean that fixed costs were £400 and variable costs were 0.5 × the number of units produced

  o If Y is, say, total daily sales in units, this might mean that 400 was, say, the number of regular standing orders and X might be the number of telephone enquiries received

---

Exam focus. In the May 1996 exam, candidates had to interpret non-linear (quadratic and logarithmic) cost functions. Such functions facilitate the incorporation of economies of scale.

Learning curves   5/99

Whenever an individual starts a job which is fairly *repetitive* in nature, and provided that his speed of working is not dictated to him by the speed of machinery, he is likely to become more *confident* and *knowledgeable* about the work as he *gains experience*, to become more *efficient*, and to do the work *more quickly.*

The basic principle of the learning curve effect is that as the number of tasks performed is doubled, the total time taken to perform the tasks is reduced by a fixed percentage.

- An 80% learning curve means that when the number of tasks performed is doubled, it should take 20% less time to perform the tasks

- A 75% learning curve means that there should be a 25% reduction in the time taken to perform twice as many tasks

---

Exam focus. In the 5/99 exam, an entire Section B question was set on the learning curve effect. You can find this question in the Year 2000 edition of BPP's MSA Practice and Revision Kit - it's Question 92. This is the only time that learning curves have been examined to date - make sure you are well prepared if it comes up again!

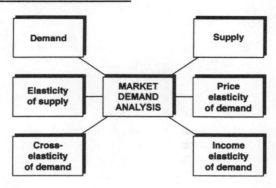

Demand

The demand curve (*price* against *quantity*) represents estimates of the quantities of a good that would be demanded per time period at different price levels.

Demand is influenced by *price*. Demand is higher at lower prices, and so the demand curve slopes downwards from left to right.

As well as price, a number of factors influence demand.

- The price and availability of *substitutes* (eg tea and coffee)

- The price and availability of *complements* (eg CD players and CDs)

- The size of household income

- Tastes, fashions, attitudes towards a good

- Consumer expectations about future market conditions (eg *expected* price rises or supply shortages)

- The distribution of income among the population

Supply

The supply curve (again, *price* against *quantity*) represents estimates of the quantities of a good that firms in the industry will want to supply to the market per time period at different price levels.

Firms will want to supply more at higher prices, and so the supply curve slopes upwards from left to right.

A change in price is reflected by a *movement along* the supply curve. A change in other supply conditions will cause a shift in the supply curve itself.

Price elasticity of demand

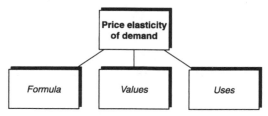

Formula

% change in quantity demanded
───────────────────────────
      % change in price

Values (ignoring sign)

0   Demand is perfectly price inelastic. Price does not affect demand (eg a vertical straight line demand curve).

0 to 1   Demand is price inelastic. A price cut causes a fall in revenue.

1   Demand has unit price elasticity. Price changes do not influence revenue.

1 to ∞ Demand is price elastic. A price cut leads to a rise in revenue.

∞   Demand is perfectly price elastic. Small rise in price reduces demand to zero (eg a horizontal straight line demand curve).

Uses

- Estimating effect on revenue of changing price

- Predicting change in volume sold if price changes

- For government, judging the effect on indirect tax revenue of change in tax on a good

Income elasticity of demand

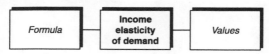

Formula

$$\frac{\text{\% change in demand}}{\text{\% change in income}}$$

Values

> 1   Demand is income elastic. This is a *normal good* where demand will grow at a greater rate than the level of income.

0 to 1   Demand is income inelastic. A normal good but demand will rise at less than the rate of income.

0   Demand has nil income elasticity. Demand will not change with income.

< 0   Demand has negative income elasticity. This is an *inferior good* where demand falls as income rises.

Cross-elasticity of demand

% change in demand for good A
────────────────────────────
% change in price of good B

The concept of cross-elasticity is used when considering substitutes and complementary products.

Elasticity of supply

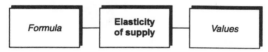

Formula

% change in quantity supplied
──────────────────────────────
% change in price

Values

0   Supply is perfectly price inelastic. Price does not affect supply, eg antiques, vintage wines (applies if supply curve is vertical).

0 to 1   Supply is price inelastic. Price changes cause smaller proportionate changes in supply.

1   Supply has unit price elasticity. Supply varies proportionately with price (applies where straight supply curve passes through origin).

1 to ∞   Supply is price elastic. A price change causes larger proportionate change in supply.

∞   Supply is perfectly price elastic. Producers will supply any amount at a given price but none at a slightly lower price (applies if supply curve is horizontal).

Exam focus. Don't just learn the formulae for PED etc and assume that is all you need to know. MSA questions are more likely to test your *understanding* of factors influencing demand or supply, the impact of complements and so on. These are all useful points to include in the written commentary parts of questions.

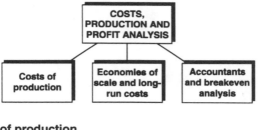

Costs of production   5/99

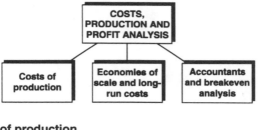

Definitions

- *Fixed costs:* costs of production that do not vary with output in the short run

- *Variable costs:* costs that do vary with output in the short run

- *Total costs:* total fixed costs + total variable costs

- *Average costs:* total costs ÷ quantity produced

- *Marginal costs:* addition to total cost from increasing output by one unit

Average cost

- Average fixed cost (AFC) is continuously falling as output grows

- Average variable cost (AVC) reaches a minimum value, and then starts to increase

- Average total cost (AC) reaches a minimum value, and then starts to increase

Law of diminishing returns

The U-shaped short-run AC curve (see the diagram below) is explained by the *law of diminishing returns* to a factor, which is as follows.

As additional units of a factor of production are employed while others are held constant, the additional output generated will eventually diminish.

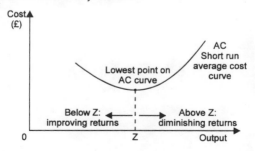

Profit maximisation

- Total profit can be measured as

    (average revenue – average cost) × quantity sold

    $$(AR - AC) \times Q$$

- A company will make extra profit by producing and selling more if marginal revenue MR exceeds MC

- Profit will be maximised when MC rises to the output level where MR = MC

Economies of scale and long-run costs   5/96

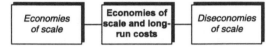

The period during which all factors of production are variable within the constraints of existing technology is called the long run.

In the long run, firms' output decisions are influenced by the possibility of *economies of scale* and *diseconomies of scale*.

Economies of scale

- Internal: resulting from growth in the size of the firm alone

- *External:* resulting from growth in the industry as a whole

Sources of internal economies of scale are as follows.

- Technical
    - Division of labour
    - Specialised machinery
    - Economies of increased dimensions

- Managerial
  - Use of specialists rather than all-rounders
  - Transfer of expertise from one area to another

- Financial
  - Cheaper finance available to larger firms
  - Ability to spread risks over a larger product range or different markets
  - Power to extract longer credit periods from suppliers

- Marketing
  - Bulk purchasing discounts
  - Discounts on bulk advertising
  - Brand name transfers across products could reduce marketing costs (eg 'Mars bar' name also used for ice cream)

Sources of external economies of scale are as follows.

- Location of ancillary services and component manufacturers near major industrial concentrations

- Government provision of education and training in growth sectors

- Creation of infrastructure

Diseconomies of scale

Sources of diseconomies of scale are as follows.

- Managerial problems in co-ordinating larger enterprises efficiently

- Increased reliance upon local input markets (eg labour) may raise factor costs (eg wages)

- Increased losses if production is held up (eg a strike on one section of an assembly line)

- Possible lower morale of staff in larger firms

Ways of limiting diseconomies of scale are as follows.

- *Replication:* increase scale by duplicating units rather than increasing size of units

- *Delegation:* allow decisions to be taken at lower levels to improve knowledge and morale

- *Autonomy:* allow parts of the enterprise greater scope to manage themselves rather than manage them all centrally

Accountants and breakeven analysis
11/95, 5/96, 11/96, 5/98, 11/98, 5/99

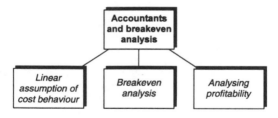

Linear assumption of cost behaviour

The economist's view of cost behaviour is represented by the following diagram.

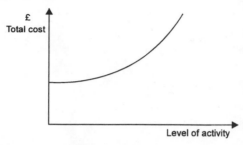

Accountants assume that costs increase in a straight line (linear) fashion as the level of activity increases. There are four main justifications for such an assumption.

- It is easier to understand

- It is easier to estimate fixed and variable costs

- The assumption is only used within normal ranges of output (relevant range)

- Within the relevant range it is sufficiently accurate

Breakeven analysis

Breakeven analysis enables management to predict how changes in volume (production output and sales) will impact upon costs and revenues and hence profitability.

	Total	Per unit
Selling price	X	X
Variable costs	(X)	(X)
Contribution	**X**	**X**
Fixed costs	(X)	(X)
Profit	X	X

- Breakeven point = activity level at which there is neither profit nor loss

$$= \frac{\text{total fixed costs}}{\text{contribution per unit}}$$

$$= \frac{\text{contribution required to breakeven}}{\text{contribution per unit}}$$

- Contribution/sales (C/S) ratio = profit/volume (P/V) ratio = (contribution/sales) × 100%

- Sales revenue at breakeven point = $\dfrac{\text{fixed costs}}{\text{C / S ratio}}$

- Margin of safety (in units)

  = budgeted sales units – breakeven sales units

  Margin of safety (as %)

$$= \frac{\text{budgeted sales} - \text{breakeven sales}}{\text{budgeted sales}} \times 100\%$$

- Sales volume to achieve a target profit

$$= \frac{\text{fixed cost} + \text{target profit}}{\text{contribution per unit}}$$

Example

Selling price	= £15 per unit
Variable cost	= £12 per unit
Fixed costs	= £5,400 per annum
Budgeted annual sales	= 3,000 units

- Breakeven point in units = $\dfrac{£5,400}{£(15-12)}$ = 1,800 units

- C/S ratio = $(3/15) \times 100\%$ = 20%

- Breakeven point in revenue = $\dfrac{£5,400}{0.2}$ = £27,000

- Sales volume to achieve profit of £3,300 =

$$\frac{£(5,400 + 3,300)}{£3} = 2,900 \text{ units}$$

- Margin of safety (as a %) = $\dfrac{3,000 - 1,800}{3,000} \times 100\%$ = 40%

Exam focus. In an examination, you may come across a question that requires you to find the breakeven position given an equation for profit in the form $ax^2 + bx + c$. Remember that breakeven occurs when profit is 0, ie when $ax^2 + bx + c = 0$. This is a quadratic equation which can be solved using the following

formula: $x = \dfrac{-b \pm \sqrt{b^2 - (4 \times a \times c)}}{2a}$

Analysing profitability

If you are asked to analyse or report on the profitability of different products, say, your answer is likely to include calculations of the following (in tabular form) in total and product by product.

- Units sold

- Turnover

- Variable costs (categorised as appropriate)

- Contribution

- Fixed costs (allocated as instructed in the question)

- Net profit

Commentary would consider whether sales and contribution are increasing, how product mix is changing, impacts on cash flow, a forecast of what is likely to happen in the future and conclusions and recommendations.

> *Exam focus.* In the November 1995 paper candidates were given total monthly sales in unit terms for a year and had to sum these and split them between products in a given ratio, apply the relevant prices and costs and allocate fixed costs. Then they had to perform similar calculations for the following year given changes in volume of sales and increases in prices and costs. The maths is very simple but it needs a cool head.

Pricing policy

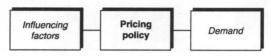

Influencing factors

Pricing policy may be influenced by the following factors.

- Price sensitivity of purchasers (eg company cars)
- Price perception (eg designer labels)
- Intermediaries' objectives (eg retailers)
- Competitors' actions and reactions
- Suppliers' prices
- Inflation
- Quality connotations
- New product pricing
- Income effects (eg recession)
- Complements, substitutes and loss leaders
- Ethics

Demand

Price is far from being the only determinant of demand, or even the main determinant.

All of the factors listed above will help to determine demand levels.

In addition it could be argued that marketing, marketing communications (sales promotion, advertising, direct selling etc), and distribution (ie physical availability) are the most important determinants in the modern environment.

The demand-based approach
5/96, 11/96, 5/97, 5/98, 11/98, 11/99

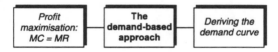

Profit maximisation: MC = MR

Following economic theory it is argued that there is an optimum price/output level at which the business can maximise its profits.

This is the price level at which the marginal cost of making an extra unit of output is equal to the marginal revenue obtained from selling it (MC = MR).

This *might* be possible if the organisation is in a monopoly position and free from all external influences, and if the information needed can be obtained and relied upon to hold true. These conditions are unlikely to occur in practice.

Deriving the demand curve

If demand is linear the equation for the demand curve is:

$$P = a - \frac{bQ}{\Delta Q}$$

where P = the price

Q = the quantity demanded

a = the price at which demand would be nil

b = the amount by which the price falls for each stepped change in demand

ΔQ = the stepped change in demand

The constant a is calculated as

$$a = £(\text{current price}) + \left(\frac{\text{Current qty at current price}}{\text{Change in qty when price is changed by £b}} \times £b \right)$$

For example, P = £10, Q = 100 units. Q falls to 95 units if P rises to £11.

a = £10 + (100/5 × 1) = £30
P = 30 − Q/5

If demand is linear, an alternative equation for the demand curve is:

$$P = a + bQ$$

where P = the price

Q = the quantity demanded

a = the price at which demand would be nil

$$b = \frac{\Delta P}{\Delta Q} = \frac{\text{change in price}}{\text{change in quantity}}$$

For example, P = £10, Q = 100 units, Q falls to 95 units if P rises to £11

$$b = \frac{\Delta P}{\Delta Q} = \frac{10-11}{100-95} = \frac{-1}{5}$$

$$\therefore \quad a = P - bQ$$

$$a = 10 - (-\frac{1}{5} \times 100)$$

$$a = 10 + 20$$

$$a = £30$$

$$\therefore \quad P = 30 - \frac{Q}{5}$$

Exam focus. In the May 1998 examination, candidates were required to derive a demand curve and calculate the breakeven positions (price and demand). There were also 5 marks available for explaining how a *spreadsheet* would be used to derive the curve and calculate the breakeven positions. Note that it is now very common for exam questions covering all aspects of the syllabus to make reference to the use of computers and spreadsheets.

Cost-based approaches   *11/95*

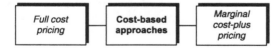

Full cost pricing

By this method the sales price is determined by calculating the full cost of the product and then adding a percentage mark-up for profit.

The full cost may be a fully absorbed production cost or it may also include some absorbed administration, selling and distribution overhead.

Some of the reasons why absorption cost tends to be used by managers in pricing decisions rather than alternative methods of costing (in particular marginal costing) are as follows.

- In the long run all costs must be recovered to stay in business and some managers believe that this is best achieved by having every product priced above its absorption, or total unit, cost

- Cost-volume analysis for individual products can be expensive to undertake whereas unit data based on absorption costing is readily available in most accounting systems at minimal cost

- There is much uncertainty about the shape of demand curves and full cost pricing copes with this uncertainty by not encouraging managers to take marginal business

- Absorption cost pricing is believed to promote price stability which in turn assists in planning

However there are problems with this approach.

- An equitable allocation of overheads is not easy to achieve: there will almost certainly be some element of subjectivity in the allocation

- Cost and activity levels rarely correspond with those budgeted and products may significantly under or over absorb overhead costs as a result

- It fails to recognise that since sales demand is partly determined by the sales price there may be a profit-maximising combination of price and demand

Marginal cost-plus pricing

A profit margin is added on to the marginal cost.

The main argument in favour of this approach is that it is more likely than full cost pricing to arrive at a profit-maximising price.

Exam focus. The main points to remember when dealing with managerial economics questions in an examination are summarised as follows.

- *Total revenue formula*

    $$TR = P \times Q$$

    where TR = Total Revenue

    P = Price

    Q = Quantity

- *Total cost formula*

    $$TC = F + VQ$$

    where TC = Total Costs

    F = Fixed costs

    V = variable cost per unit

    Q = Quantity

- *Profit maximisation*

    Profits are maximised when

    $$MC = MR$$

    where MC = marginal cost (=V unless told otherwise)

    MR = marginal revenue

- *Revenue Maximisation*

    Revenue is maximised when

    $$MR = 0$$

- *Total profit formula*

    $$Profit = TR - TC$$

- *Breakeven profits*

    Profit = TR − TC = 0 at the breakeven point

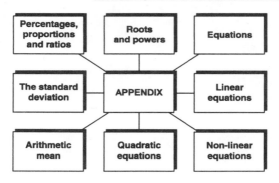

Percentages, proportions and ratios

Percentages

To turn a percentage into a fraction or a decimal you divide by 100%.

$$40\% = \frac{40\%}{100\%} = \frac{4}{10} = \frac{2}{5} = 0.4$$

To turn a fraction or decimal into a percentage you multiply by 100%.

$$\frac{3}{5} = \frac{3 \times 100\%}{5} = 60\%$$

$$0.16 = 0.16 \times 100\% = 16\%$$

You may have to deal with other problems involving percentages.

- $40\% \times 64 = 0.4 \times 64 = 25.6$

- 16 as a percentage of 64 $= \dfrac{16}{64} \times 100\% = \dfrac{1}{4} \times 100\% = 25\%$

- VAT element of something costing £35.25 in total $=$ $17.5/117.5 \times £35.25 = £5.25$

Proportions

A proportion is another way of indicating the relative size of something. Suppose there is 1 man in a group of 5 people.

- $1/5$ is the *fraction* of the group made up by men

- 20% is the *percentage* of the group made up by men

- 0.2 is the *proportion* of the group made up by men

Ratios

Annabel and Bert want to share £100 in the ratio 3:2. How much will each receive?

Number of parts $= 3 + 2 = 5$

Value of each part $= \dfrac{£100}{5} = £20$

Annabel's share $= 3 \times £20 = £60$, Bert's share $= 2 \times £20 = £40$.

Roots and powers

The nth root of a number is the value which, when multiplied by itself $(n-1)$ times, equals the original number.

The nth power of a number is the value given when the original number is multiplied by itself $(n-1)$ times.

The rules of arithmetic with powers and roots are as follows.

- $5^3 \times 5^7 = 5^{3+7} = 5^{10}$
- $3^6 \div 3^2 = 3^{6-2} = 3^4$
- $10^0 = 1$; $357^0 = 1$; $10,394^0 = 1$
- $7^{1/2}$ = square root of 7; $11^{1/3}$ = cube root of 11; $27^{1/9}$ = 9th root of 27
- $4^{-1} = {}^1/4^1 = {}^1/4$; $5^{-6} = {}^1/5^6 = {}^1/15{,}625$
- $3^4 \times 3^{-2} = 3^4 \times {}^1/3^2 = 3^{4+-2} = 3^2 = 9$
- $2^6 \div 2^{-2} = 2^{6--2} = 2^8$
- $4^{-4} \div 4^{-2} = 4^{-4--2} = 4^{-2} = {}^1/4^2 = {}^1/16$

Equations

To solve an equation we need to get it into the form:

unknown variable (such as x) = something with numbers in it which we can work out

To do this, follow the rule that you can do what you like to one side of an equation (such as divide by 100) as long as you do it to the other side straightaway.

$$
\begin{aligned}
450 &= 3x + 72 \\
450 - 72 &= 3x \qquad \text{(subtract 72 from both sides)} \\
\frac{450 - 72}{3} &= x \qquad \text{(divide each side by 3)} \\
126 &= x
\end{aligned}
$$

Linear equations

General form

A linear equation has the general form $y = a + bx$

where   y is the dependent variable (depends on value of x)
x is the independent variable (determines value of y)
a and b are constants

Linear equations and graphs

The graph of a linear equation is a straight line and is determined by two things.

- The gradient (or slope) of the straight line = b in the general form of a linear equation
  - If $b > 0$ the gradient is positive and slopes *upwards* from left to right
  - If $b < 0$ the gradient is negative and slopes *downwards* from left to right
  - If $b = 0$ the line is horizontal
  - The greater the value of b, the steeper the gradient
  - Gradient of the graph of a linear equation

    $= (y_2 - y_1)/(x_2 - x_1)$, where (x_1, y_1), (x_2, y_2) are two points on the straight line

- The point at which the straight line crosses the y (vertical) axis = a in the general form of a linear equation = the intercept

- Example: $5y = 20x - 15 \Rightarrow y = 4x - 3$

  Gradient (b) = 4 and intercept (a) = −3

Simultaneous linear equations

Simultaneous linear equations are two or more equations which are satisfied by the same variable values. To find the values of unknown variables you need as many equations as there are unknowns.

- Graphical solution: plot the equations on one graph and find their intersection point

- Algebraic solution

  Example: $y = 6x + 32$ (1)

  $2y = 2x + 144$ (2)

  $2y = 12x + 64$ (3) ((1) × 2)

  $0 = 10x - 80$ (3) − (2)

  $x = 8$ and $y = 48 + 32 = 80$

Non-linear equations

Linear equations are those in which the highest power of the unknown variable(s) is (are) one.

Non-linear equations are those in which one variable varies with the nth power of another, where $n > 1$. They can be expressed in the form $y = ax^n + bx^{n-1} + cx^{n-2} + ... + constant$.

The graph of a linear equation is a straight line. The graph of a non-linear equation is not.

Quadratic equations

General form

A quadratic equation is a type of non-linear equation in which one variable varies with the square (or second power) of the other variable. It may also include a term involving the first power of the other variable.

The general form of a quadratic equation is $y = ax^2 + bx + c$.

Graphing quadratic equations

The graph of $y = ax^2 + bx + c$ forms a type of curve known as a parabola.

- 'c' determines the value of y at the point where the curve crosses the y axis

- The sign of 'a' determines the way up the curve appears
  - If $a > 0$, curve is ditch shaped and has a minimum point
  - If $a < 0$, curve is bell shaped and has a maximum point

- Graph shows the solution (if any) of $0 = ax^2 + bx + c$ (the values for x when $y = 0$)

Solving quadratic equations

For any value of y, most quadratic equations have two solutions for x or 'roots of the equation'. If $ax^2 + bx + c = 0$ then the roots $= \dfrac{-b \pm \sqrt{b^2 - 4ac}}{2a}$.

Example: $x^2 + x - 4 = -2$

$\therefore \; x^2 + x - 2 = 0$

$$x = \frac{-1 \pm \sqrt{\left(1 - \left(4 \times 1 \times -2\right)\right)}}{2}$$

$$= \frac{-1 \pm \sqrt{9}}{2}$$

$$= 1 \text{ or } -2$$

Some quadratic equations (such as $x^2 + 2x + 1 = 0$) have only one root.

Arithmetic mean

- Arithmetic mean for ungrouped data

  $$\bar{x} = \frac{\text{Sum of value of items}}{\text{Number of items}} = \frac{\Sigma x}{n}$$

- Arithmetic mean for data in a frequency distribution

  $$\bar{x} = \frac{\Sigma fx}{n} = \frac{\Sigma fx}{\Sigma f}$$

- *Estimate* of mean of a grouped frequency distribution

  $$\bar{x} = \frac{\Sigma fx}{\Sigma f} \text{ (where x is the midpoint of each class interval)}$$

- Advantages
  - Widely understood
  - Value of every item included in the computation
  - Supported by mathematical theory and suited to further statistical analysis

- Disadvantages
  - Value of mean may not correspond to an actual value
  - Distorted by extremely high or low values

The standard deviation

- Most important measure of spread

  $$SD = \sqrt{\frac{\Sigma(x - \bar{x})^2}{n - 1}} \text{ or } \sqrt{\frac{\Sigma(x - \bar{x})^2}{n}} \text{ if n is large}$$

  $$SD = \sqrt{\frac{\Sigma fx^2}{\Sigma f} - \bar{x}^2} \text{ (frequency distribution)}$$

- Standard deviation = $\sqrt{variance}$

- Standard deviation of a sample = s

- Standard deviation of a population = σ

- Main properties
  - Uses all values in the distribution
  - Suitable for further statistical analysis
  - More difficult to understand than some other measures

- Standard deviation of N items together, given standard deviations for each item (SD_1, SD_2, ..., SD_N) =

$$\sqrt{\left(SD_1^2 + SD_2^2 + ... SD_N^2\right)}$$